Lions in the wild

Cliff Moon

Wayland

In the Wild

Elephants in the Wild
Lions in the Wild

Further titles are in preparation

*This book is based on an original text
by Mary Chipperfield.*

First published in 1984 by
Wayland (Publishers) Ltd
49 Lansdowne Place, Hove
East Sussex BN3 1HF, England

ISBN 0 85078 374 7

Phototypeset by
Kalligraphics Ltd, Redhill, Surrey
Printed in Italy by
G. Canale & C.S.p.A., Turin
Bound in the UK by
The Pitman Press, Bath

Contents

Lions

Have you ever seen a lion?
You can see lions in a zoo,
a circus or a safari park.
Lions like safari parks
because they can live there
just as they do in the wild.
Long ago there were more lions
than there are now.
People came to the places
where they lived and
started to farm the land.

These lions are lucky.
The place where they live
is not being farmed.
But where do lions live
in the wild?

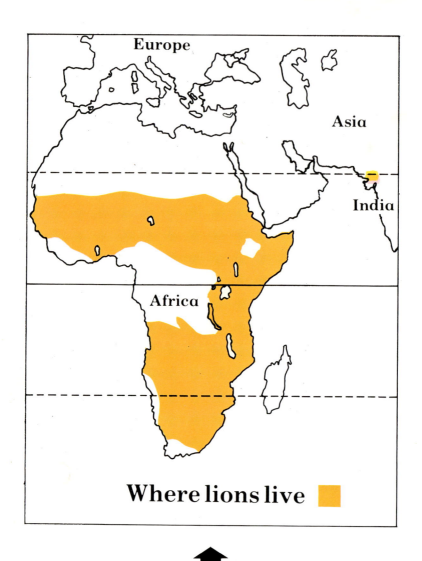

Europe

Asia

India

Africa

Where lions live

As you can see from this map
most wild lions live in Africa.
There is one small part of India
called the **Forest of Gir**
where about 300 lions live.

Here are some of the animals
that lions hunt for food.
There are zebras and wildebeests
but lions also eat giraffes.
These animals move about in herds
and the lions follow them.

This is an Indian lion.
The long hair around his neck
is called a **mane**.

Here is an African lion.
He is a bit bigger than
an Indian lion and
his mane is longer.

Lions need long sharp teeth
when they hunt for animals
to kill and eat.

A male lion has a mane.
A female lion has no mane
and she is a bit smaller
than a male.
They are both the same colour
as the yellow sandy soil and
the dry grass.

What is it that both male and
female lions have on their tails?
(Answer on page 54)

These lions live together
in a group called a **pride**.
There are between 5 and 30 lions
in a pride.

Tigers and leopards like to live
on their own and even lions
often hunt on their own so
no one really knows why
lions live in prides.
When a lion kills an animal
the other lions in the pride
share the meal.
There are male lions, female lions
and baby lions in a pride.

Do you know what baby lions
are called?
(Answer on page 54)

Life in the Wild

Lions are very lazy!
They like to sleep for about
20 hours every day.
They usually hunt at night but
male lions often look after the cubs
and let the females go hunting.
Female lions can run, jump and
hide better than males
because they are smaller and
thinner and have no manes.

These lions have just hunted
and killed a zebra.
Now they will eat it.

Every year an African lion
kills between 20 and 30 animals.
But this helps the animals
because if they all lived
there would not be enough grass
for them to eat and
many would starve to death.

How much meat do you think
a lion eats in a day?
(Answer on page 54)

These female lions are drinking
at a water-hole.
They look for food as they drink.

Lions roar to tell the pride
where they are or to warn
other prides to stay away.
If there are too many prides
in one place there will not
be enough food to go round.

How are birds like lions?
(Answer on page 54)

This lion has climbed a tree
to have a rest among
the cool leaves and branches.

Lions do not climb very often.
They are too big and heavy
to be good climbers.
Lions do not jump down
onto an animal to kill it.
They hide in bushes and
creep along quietly until
they are close enough.
Then they leap out and
kill the animal.

Food for Lions

The lions have slept all day.
They woke up at sunset and
went hunting and now
they are enjoying their meal.

This lion is looking for food.
She will creep through the grass
very quietly until she finds
an animal to kill.

The lion has found her meal.
She may kill two animals
in one night but sometimes
she is not so lucky and
may have to wait a few days
for her next meal.

After the lion has eaten
she shares the meat
with the other lions and
lion cubs in her pride.
The cubs come last and
eat up all the left-overs.

Female lions are very clever
when they hunt animals.
Some other lions are waiting
in the bushes and this lion
chases the zebras towards them.

Why do you think lions
catch other animals like this?
(Answer on page 55)

This lion is creeping up quietly
on an animal.
When she gets close enough
she will jump on the animal.
Perhaps she will bite its throat
to kill it or she will jump
from behind and break its back.

A lion cub cannot eat a giraffe
all by himself!
Some of the other lions
will soon come to help him out.

If a lion kills a small animal
she will eat it all herself.
When a big animal is killed
all the lions grab some meat
and take it away to eat
on their own.

The cubs eat last of all and
sometimes there is nothing left.
But the biggest male in the pride
might help them.
Do you know what he does?
(Answer on page 55)

Hyenas like this follow the lions
and eat up the bones and scraps
which they leave behind
when they have killed an animal.

Sometimes a pack of hyenas
will kill an animal and then
the lions come along and
eat it for them!

Jackals also eat the scraps
after a lion has finished eating.
This jackal will wait until
the lion has gone away.

Jackals are not like hyenas
because they do not kill animals
themselves – they only eat
what the lions leave behind.

Lion Cubs

 A lion cub looks as gentle
as a kitten but his teeth
are growing stronger and
his claws are getting sharper.

Lions look after their cubs
just as we look after our babies.

39

These cubs are drinking milk
from their mother.

Cubs are born about 16 weeks
after their mother has mated
with a male lion.
A female lion can have one,
two, three, four or five cubs
at the same time.
She keeps them very safe
in a hole or a cave and
other lions in the pride
come to see them.
Lion cubs cannot see until
they are about 2 weeks old
because their eyes are closed
when they are born.

How do you think the lion
will carry her cubs
if they are in danger?
(Answer on page 55)

These cubs are a few weeks old.
They can walk now but
sometimes they fall over!
The lions in a pride try
to look after their cubs
but many die because
they do not get enough to eat.

This female lion is sad.
She went hunting but
when she got back her cubs
had been killed by a lion
from another pride.

Cubs like to romp and play
just like kittens.
They jump on the lions' tails
and climb on their backs.
The female lions do not mind
but the males get fed up and
hit the cubs with their paws.

The cubs stay behind
when the lions go hunting.
The lions eat first and
fetch the cubs later
when they have finished.

Lions and People

Lions are very beautiful.
They look strong and brave
and they move like cats.
Long ago hunters shot them
and took their heads home
to show their friends.
Nowadays we do not shoot lions.
We look after them so that
they can live safely in the wild.

People go to Africa to see
animals living in the wild.
This woman is taking a photo
of a pride of lions
in a game park.

There are many game parks
all over Africa.
Game wardens look after
all the birds and animals
in the game parks.
They make sure that no one
shoots them and that they have
enough to eat and drink.

Why do you think that
African countries have set up
so many game parks?
(Answer on page 55)

Some people go to game parks
for their holidays but
other people go there to work.
They are good places to study
animals in the wild.

These lions are having a rest.
When they wake up they will be hungry
and they won't have far to go
for their next meal!

Answers to Questions

Page 11
Both male and female lions
have a dark tip at the end
of their tails.

Page 13
Baby lions are called **cubs**.

Page 19
A lion eats about 7 kg (15 lb)
of meat every day –
about 50 times more than you eat!

Page 22
Birds are like lions because
they whistle and sing to warn
other birds to stay away.
If there are too many birds
in one place there will not be
enough food to go round.

Page 32
Lions chase animals and trap them
because they are not very good
at running fast for a long time.

Page 35
When there is no meat left
the biggest male in the pride
shares his meat with the cubs.

Page 40
A lion carries a cub by
grasping the back of its neck
in her mouth.
This is what cats do
when they carry kittens.

Page 51
African countries have set up
game parks so that people
will go for holidays and
spend money there.

Index

Picture Acknowledgements
The illustrations in this book were supplied by: Bruce Coleman *front cover*, 7, 14–15, 22, 32, 38, 46–7, 48 (top); Ecology Pictures 11, 37, 39, 48–9; N.H.P.A. *endpapers*, 4, 8, 9, 10, 12, 16, 17, 18, 20–21, 23, 24, 26–7, 28, 29, 30, 31, 33, 34, 36, 41, 42, 43, 45, 50, 52–3; and Michael Paysden 6.

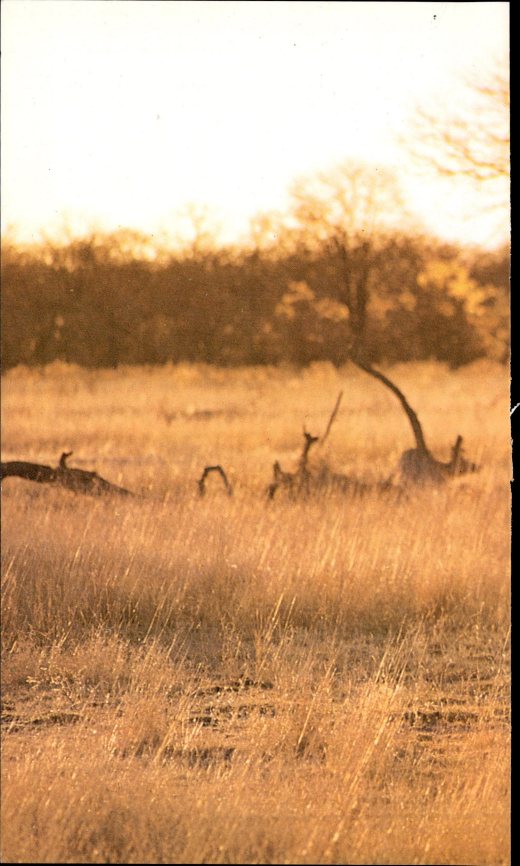